Tuba

BRASS ON BROADWAY

arranged for brass quintet
by Bob Lowden

intermediate   level

THE CANADIAN BRASS

CANADIAN BRASS
SERIES OF
COLLECTED QUINTETS

BROADWAY BABY

(From *FOLLIES*)

TUBA

Words and Music by
Stephen Sondheim

COMEDY TONIGHT

From *A FUNNY THING HAPPENED ON THE WAY TO THE FORUM*

TUBA

Words and Music by
Stephen Sondheim

Bright in 2 (♩ = 120)

GET ME TO THE CHURCH ON TIME

(From *My Fair Lady*)

TUBA

Words by Alan Jay Lerner
Music by Frederick Loewe

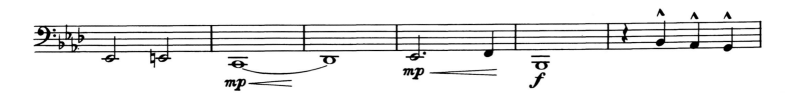

OL' MAN RIVER
(From *SHOW BOAT*)

TUBA

Words by Oscar Hammerstein II
Music by Jerome Kern

SUNRISE, SUNSET
(From *FIDDLER ON THE ROOF*)

TUBA

Words by Sheldon Harnick
Music by Jerry Bock

CANADIAN
BRASS
SERIES OF
COLLECTED QUINTETS

BRASS ON BROADWAY

arranged for brass quintet
by Bob Lowden

contents

Welcome to the *Canadian Brass Series of Collected Quintets*. In our work with students, for some time we have been aware of the need for more brass quintet music at easy and intermediate levels of difficulty. We are continually observing a kind of "Renaissance" in brass music, not only in audience responses to our quintet, but to all brass music in general. The brass quintet, as a chamber ensemble, seems to have become as standard a chamber combination as a string quartet. That could not have been said twenty-five years ago. Brass quintets are popping up everywhere — professional quintets, junior and senior high school ensembles, college and university groups, and amateur quintets of adult players.

We have carefully chosen the literature for these collected quintets, and closely supervised the arrangements. Our aim was to retain a Canadian Brass flavor to each arrangement, and create attractive repertory designed so that any brass quintet can play it with satisfying results. We've often remarked to one another that we certainly wish that we'd had quintet arrangements like these when we were students!

Happy playing to you and your quintet.

— THE CANADIAN BRASS

0-73999-88782-2

U.S. $9.99

ISBN 978-1-4584-0170-0

50488782

HAL•LEONARD®
CORPORATION
7777 W. BLUEMOUND RD. P.O. BOX 13819 MILWAUKEE, WI 53213